SECOND BOOK

of

PRACTICAL STUDIES

for

CORNET and TRUMPET

by

Robert W. Getchell

Edited by

NILO W. HOVEY

ED. LIBR.
No. 305

Foreword

This SECOND BOOK OF PRACTICAL STUDIES is designed to logically extend the techniques already presented in the FIRST BOOK and also to introduce and develop new techniques and rhythms that will offer a challenge to the intermediate student. Through the use of slightly more difficult and more extended studies, it is hoped that the material included in this book may more fully develop general musicianship and more feeling for style and interpretation and thus act as a foundation for solo literature.

The following rhythms are introduced and developed in this Second Book.

ED. LIBR.
No. 305

65

66

67

E.L. 305

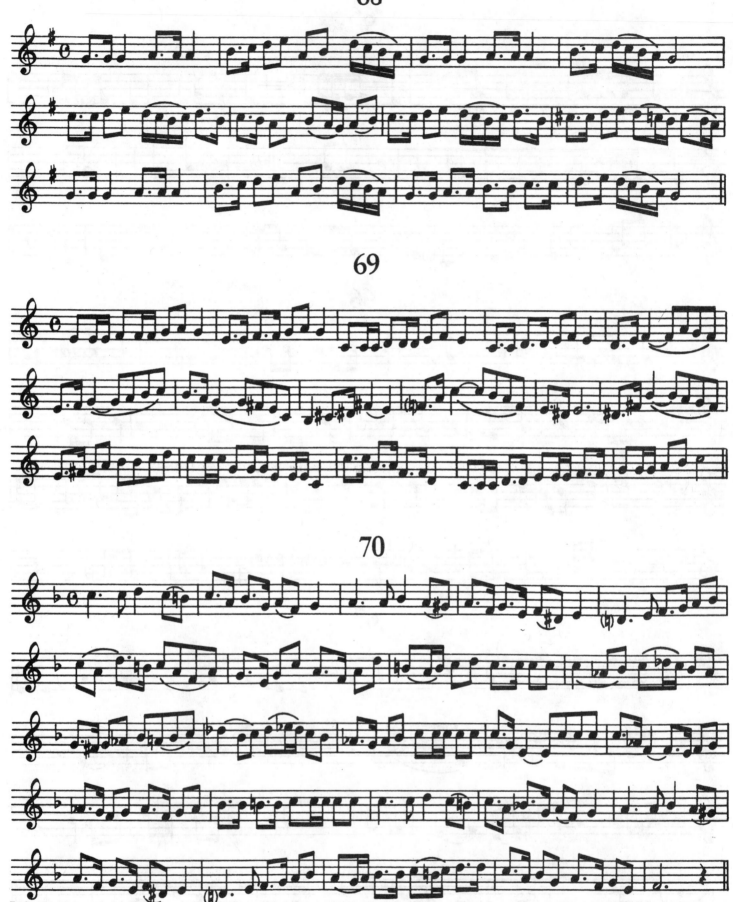

71

72

73

74

Moderato

75

Allegro

76

Allegretto

77

Grandioso

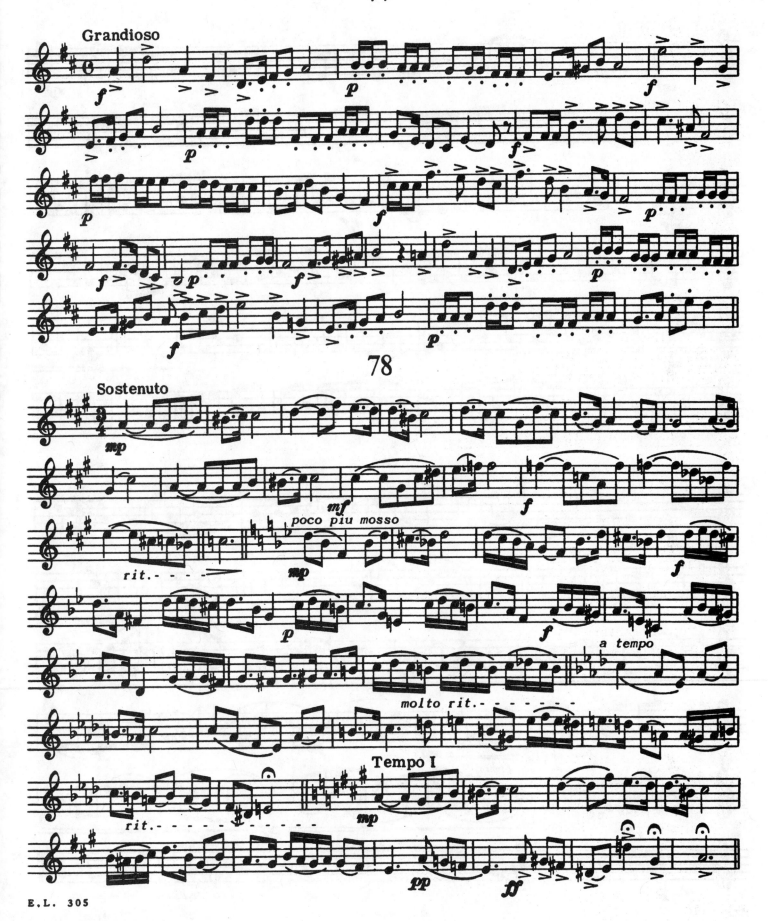

78

Sostenuto

79

Giocoso

80

Religioso - very slow

81

82

83

84

85

88

89

90

Andante cantabile

91

Andantino

92

93

94

95

96

97

Largo espressivo

mp

rit.

a tempo

piu mosso

cresc.- - - - - - - - - - - - - - - f *dim.- - - rit.- - - - - - -*

Tempo I

mp

(broadly)

cresc.- - - - - - - - - - f *dim.- - - - - - - - - p*

98

Giocoso

mf

99

100

101

102

Andantino

103

Cantabile (in 2)

(simile)

cresc. - - - - - - - - - - - - - - - - - - - mf

104

105

106

107

108

109

110

58

111

112

114

115

116

117

118

119

120

121

TO THE STUDENT: The care with which a player "warms up" prior to a rehearsal or a practice session plays a very important part in determining how successfully his embouchure will respond. A thorough warm-up routine is especially important before the <u>initial</u> practice session each day.

Intonation, tone-quality, range and endurance are all affected by a careful warm-up which has the effect of flexing the lip muscles and preparing them for the day's work.

Following is a suggested routine that may be followed although variations of any of the following exercises are also recommended:

I. Mouthpiece Drill. This includes buzzing long tones of various pitches with the mouthpiece alone. Also, slurring over intervals as follows:

It is suggested that this procedure take at least 2 or 3 minutes before using the instrument.

II. Long Tones. Care should be taken that a uniform pitch and quality be maintained at all dynamic levels. Also, play in all registers within your range.

III. Octave Slurs. Strive for a uniform quality and dynamic level in all registers and do not increase volume to insure response of the upper register. Listen carefully to assure a balanced intonation in all octaves.

IV. Lip Slur Exercises. To be played as relaxed as possible and not loud. Do not resort to more volume to make the pitch go higher but make the lip and diaphragm do the work. These are only some suggestions and should be supplemented with either exercises of your own or from some of the fine books which concentrate on lip exercises.